Secrets to invest in cryptocurrencies

Content

What are cryptocurrencies 5

Types of cryptocurrencies 6

The world of cryptocurrencies and the legal aspect 7

Cryptocurrency markets today 10

What to avoid when investing in cryptocurrencies 13

Tips on cryptocurrency investment 19

How cryptocurrency trading strategies work 23

Components of a cryptocurrency trading strategy 24

How to buy cryptocurrencies 26

How to mine cryptocurrencies 27

The profitability of mining cryptocurrencies 29

Best cryptocurrency trading strategies 29

How to trade in cryptocurrency investment 37

The most used cryptocurrency investment strategies in 2021 39

How leverage is used on the investment 44

Steps for cryptocurrency trading 45

Tricks to be part of trading 47

The psychology of trading 49

How to trade cryptocurrencies, step by step 54

Types of trading 56

What you should know about Exchanges 58

How to choose the best casa da cambio for investment 60

The best Exchanges to buy and invest in cryptocurrencies 62

Prediction markets to consider in 2021 66

The diversity of cryptocurrencies 69

The most profitable cryptocurrencies 71

Which investment to choose in the world of cryptocurrencies? 73

The advantages and disadvantages of investing in cryptoassets 74

The best demo brokers 78

Alternative methods to earn money with cryptocurrencies 81

Secrets to invest in cryptocurrencies

The popularity of cryptocurrencies increases year after year, but the truth is that this preference is supported by the number of people who invest, and generate income with great success, so it is a sector to which to devote attention to take advantage of the opportunities it postulates in the economic plane.

But if you still don't know or don't know what an Ethereum or Tether is, there is no reason to worry, most only have more proximity or knowledge about Bitcoin, but in reality there are more than 1000 cryptocurrencies in the world, each with a different concept, but all are decentralized, volatile and open to active transaction.

What are cryptocurrencies

The definition of cryptocurrency is a virtual currency, it has a large digital extension, but it lacks physical presentation, since it uses cryptography, being the way through which transactions are generated and managed, in the same way, all kinds of currencies are constantly emerging.

The main qualities of a cryptocurrency start by having physical support, but it is virtual liquidity, for that reason they cannot be stored in physical devices of any kind, on the other hand the cryptography is responsible for creating units and is not controlled by any kind of government.

The main operation of this medium is based on blockchain technology, being useful to generate more and more units, it is essential to highlight that the amount of units of this currency is limited.

Types of cryptocurrencies

There are a lot of cryptocurrencies, from Dash, Ethereum, Litecoin, and much more, although most only know the popularity of Bitcoin, the difference between each one is the type of philosophy they have, all generally use blockchain technology, but with the changes it becomes more efficient to process.

Some cryptocurrencies, use very different currency formulas, such as some have an infinite number of circulation, while others do not perform or apply this measure, the same applies to the transparency of transactions, so when investing it is necessary to apply financial knowledge of these areas.

The world of cryptocurrencies and the legal aspect

First of all, the concept behind cryptocurrencies is essential, they are digital currencies, which consist of a cryptography that generates a reliable means of payment, this causes that questions may arise about the operation of the same, as well as some kind of law that protects their use, to consider the risks.

When thinking about investing in any cryptocurrency, it is essential to study every detail about the risks, as well as the type of investment you are willing to make, as this is key to make each step safely, so you can adjust to the requirements and mechanisms behind each cryptocurrency.

Each time legal and fiscal regulations are advancing over the world of cryptocurrencies, as the use of these currencies advances and has spread in different areas, but in each occasion one must be careful with that characteristic of volatility that is part of them, and in many ways it is still a developing market.

The best example of the economic changes that cryptocurrencies undergo is evidenced in the 20% that each of the coins can decline, that is to say, in the same way in which they rise, they can also fall, therefore each operation must be measured.

- **Regulation imposed on cryptocurrencies**

The authorities do not have any intervention on cryptocurrencies, but the European Commission keeps designing methods through which this aspect can be regulated, especially for a direct control of the cryptoasset markets, so that both the consumer and the investor can count on legal certainty.

This vision of regulation that is behind cryptocurrencies seeks to classify those that are considered as safe or legal, and will be considered as electronic money, which is why they will be regulated by the expert authorities in Europe.

Given the lack of regulation, transactions with cryptocurrencies have been related to the blocking of capital, something that cannot be completely denied, especially with the Bitcoin, but it is not the main or only means to carry out these plans, because even banking institutions have lent themselves to it.

For this reason, within the agenda of the European Commission, the study of money laundering is included, which seeks to force each exchanges to remain under regulation, or that is what is aspired, in the money laundering regulation, the function of exchanges has been thought of, to cover this aspect.

These considerations are motivations included on the draft Law on Measures to Prevent and Combat Tax Fraud, which has scope of action in Spain, in addition it has an initial wording dating back to Law 7/2012, seeking an incorporation of control over that aspect of virtual currencies.

- **Cryptocurrencies and the relationship with central banks**

At present, the launch of cryptocurrencies by central banks is eagerly awaited, in this regard the Central Bank of China is one of the most advanced in this area, as it has a solid project behind its cryptocurrency DC/EP, while the European Central Bank, still shows no signs of following this path.

Once the Central Bank of any country gets involved with the world of cryptocurrencies, a direct change on business models as well as on public management is originated, causing a different relationship between individuals, and on the administration, it is a revolution that must be well studied.

Cryptocurrency markets today

Since 2009 when Bitcoin emerged, it opened a big door to a world of extensive investment opportunities on more cryptocurrencies, so in 2013 it became a market full of investors, so in 2020 it is estimated that there are up to 2000 cryptocurrencies as an investment opportunity.

The capitalization that is part of this market, becomes a great reason to be part of these measures, it is a large-scale business that came to put in motion up to hundreds of billions, with a great proximity to the billions, it is a medium that has many alternatives for participation.

To this scale of the market, the technology known as Blockchain is added, being a security offering, which helps to grow the popularity of this investment medium, it is a novelty that has settled completely, but it is usual that there are doubts about the investment lapses, these deserve an analysis of what they imply.

- **Long-term investments in cryptocurrencies**

It refers to a type of investment that is practiced waiting for a change in price over time, being a simple position, usually that preference for a cryptocurrency or movement, is held for

6 months to a year to get that classification, it all depends on personal claims.

Some users may seek an investment of up to 10 years, that is at personal discretion, as well as developed in stages, or if practiced on a single direct action, this allows to pursue specific objectives, such as estimating the price to expect to sell the crypto.

In addition to this vision, it is important to know whether the sale will be carried out at different times or partially, as well as whether the company is willing to change to a short-term investment in the face of complications, i.e. in some cases it is possible to innovate with a change of strategy, for which a thorough investigation must be carried out.

The issues to check before deciding on a long-term investment are whether there is a solid team to back up the investment, whether it has a useful price-rising technology, the ability you have to research a crypto, and whether your concept is aimed at solving a real-world problem.

Before investing, it is a requirement to be convinced of its potential, so that later there are no regrets, the reasons for choosing this modality is that the investor has greater peace of mind to not closely follow the fluctuation, it is a lower level of stress, in addition to the level of possible profits to be achieved.

- **Short-term investment in cryptocurrencies**

Within a short term investment, it is essential to remember that these are short periods of time, to be in search of quick profits, the periods that are frequently used are seconds, minutes, days, weeks and in rare cases even months.

The operation of this type of investment is developed by answering the issues of the amount of losses that the investor is willing to face, because sudden drops are usual scenarios within this world, there is also the fact of measuring the benefits to be reaped, and patience is required to investigate well each step to take.

The ability to closely follow technical analysis, becomes a priority focus, because the usual characteristics of this medium is a large volume of operations, it also faces a low market capitalization, and the impact of social networks on these movements is essential.

- **How to choose to invest short or long term in cryptocurrencies**

To determine whether it is more convenient to choose a short or long term investment, there is no magic formula, but it depends directly on the type of objectives you have, in addition to previous experience in the world of cryptocurrencies, so when it comes to planning a project, it is best to think long term.

On the other hand, when it is based on a vision or follow up for new cryptocurrencies in the market, it combines much more with a short term investment, although it is a riskier path, but they are still good ideas to obtain income, because there is no doubt about the potential of cryptocurrencies to generate money.

The detail that prevails over any way, is that you can lose money, it is a world that has no written rules, there is no way to foresee the movements with certainty, the only key premise is to invest money that you are not afraid of losing, that is what you should keep in mind.

What to avoid when investing in cryptocurrencies

In a modern world where every person is actively talking about and using cryptocurrencies, it is established as a type of financial freedom that should not be missed, so it is worth educating yourself about this area, without overlooking certain mistakes that are made daily on a variety of platforms.

But the important thing is that within the learning process, the monetization of each action is not lost sight of, so that no money is lost under this planning, because as Warrent Buffett indicates, rule number 1 is not to lose money, and rule number 2 is not to forget the first rule, this is a premise of maintaining realism.

- **Do not invest in the first site you find**

It is very easy to lose money when investing without identifying security, the cryptocurrency sector has a large number of websites, for this reason one aspect to protect is the license to operate freely with each function, it is a detail on which not to make a mistake, otherwise everything is completely lost.

Once cryptocurrencies have become fashionable, it creates a big gap for scammers to take advantage with fake messages, it is an impulse that seeks to spread over users with little information, and you should not fall into this kind of trap, no matter what kind of amount you are going to deposit.

To put aside these problems, it is crucial to look for a much safer investment, causing you to be part of a totally legal business, and do not seek to run away from the issue of commissions, but the essential thing is that your money can not disappear, because instead of going to your wallet, it goes to the creator of the website.

In addition to advertisements, also many phone calls can be used to promote websites, and cryptocurrency purchases, when in the end they are a scam, that kind of scam percentages can be set aside with a role skepticism, control is useful to not make impulse purchases that are regretted.

- **Invest in a course to learn about cryptocurrencies**

For the steps within the world of cryptocurrencies to be reliable, it is vital to invest in yourself, it never hurts, every piece of information in the end you can use it to generate more money, every decision that puts your money at risk, needs a high degree of awareness, otherwise you notice that others are successful and you are not.

Ignoring the subject of learning, or trying to advance on your own, only causes you to waste a lot of time, and in investment matters this is not considered profitable, so as long as you master each piece of knowledge you need, you will be on your way to an effective resolution of profitable results.

But it cannot be just any training, you should look for courses that are ratified, and that the speakers can demonstrate their results, the essential thing is that you keep learning constantly, also avoiding that these learning alternatives keep your money.

Instead of looking for a learning method that only tells you what you want to hear, it is better to look for a means that is a challenge for you, in addition to avoiding those misleading advertisements where they teach you how to multiply your money quickly.

- **Avoid buying in the face of unfounded forecasts**

When feelings are involved in the issue of buying and investing in cryptocurrencies, the result ends up being negative, so many times in a market good times or predictions to invest are announced, but they are only positions that seek to take advantage of the greed of users.

It is easy to attract people when concepts are taught, such as those that indicate that some cryptocurrency is going to rise without stopping, since it can be easy money, but in reality it is an easy path, and the market may be looking to generate those movements to benefit from the buying and selling of the asset.

Every investment market has its upside bubble, as well as a downside where you can easily lose money, for that reason you should always be careful with every estimate or situation, especially when you can not predict the future, the value is impossible to control with certainty, above any promise.

- **Don't choose loans as an impetus to invest in cryptocurrencies**

A classic rule to follow under the movement or investment measures, is not to invest what you may need in the future, for that reason, getting into debt is not recommended to be part of the cryptocurrency movement, otherwise the results can be fatal, even if the cryptocurrency is very promising.

Thinking that you are going to earn more money, and seek a loan to reach the investment, is not the most positive thing, because if the move or choice goes wrong, you will not be able to pay the loan, you will have earned a debt, this in each case, varies, because it can go well and pay off the outstanding money, or worsen the situation completely.

- **Do not buy at a low price hoping that they will go up and become a millionaire.**

In the middle of the market there are a large number of cryptocurrencies that are not very well known, these are chosen without inquiring simply for their value, to maintain a long-term investment until they increase, but it is not a rule to take into account, because not all cryptocurrencies increase in the same way or reach an optimal value.

To avoid this, it is necessary to know what is behind the cryptocurrency, especially when not much time has elapsed since its launch, and it is more likely to wait even if they increase by 10%, instead of having aspirations that it will increase 10 times more.

- **Do not buy without measure**

To be operating blindly, making decisions without knowledge, is a serious mistake, especially given the statistic that more than 485 companies in the world disappear in a year, especially when a bubble effect is triggered, which is frequent with the daily exit of cryptocurrencies.

Buying cryptocurrencies without sense, does not generate any kind of guarantee, because the most usual thing is that this investment does not reach any productive point, without forgetting that some of these virtual currencies are based on a scam, that is why the study on their creators is the best protection not to get carried away.

- **Don't invest without knowing what you are doing**

In order not to lose money, it is essential to study and understand what you are doing, no matter if someone else advises you to buy, or if they call you, what is vital is to dedicate yourself to each financial information, and to follow the options of the platform with which you operate, to act in this way, it takes a lot of preparation.

Tips on cryptocurrency investment

Decision making in cryptocurrency investment plays a key role to get far in this environment, although to be successful in this environment also involves the action or effect of different factors, one of them is discipline, trust, and the use of risk management tools.

By being aware of this type of details that are underestimated, you can take advantage of the potential that is part of cryptocurrencies, to reach an optimal level, you need to develop the following actions:

1. Research on coins

The information you have about cryptocurrencies is decisive, the more details you can know, the better for the investor, it is necessary to have time to get to know enough, also every new development of blockchain technology is also useful, without losing sight of the trends of financial markets.

Understanding every aspect about the cryptocurrency you are trading is fundamental, to get to that level, you must maintain a continuous research, as markets evolve faster and faster, and after every event, they impose a response or movement, so it is a technical development training.

2. Design a trading plan

To form a trading plan is based on a comprehensive study where the operations are reflected, to this are added the details of response to risks, in addition to the objectives pursued from the beginning, so you can choose between one strategy and another, without forgetting to establish rules for risk management.

In the midst of this planning, you can also establish the details about a market, that way you can operate with greater fluency, it is a constant development of skills, to have a vision attached to the incidences of the market.

3. **Training in trading**

To gain experience in cryptocurrency trading, there is nothing more satisfying than to carry out a training, you can start with a demo account, so that you get to learn every option, every reading that the platform has, and this helps to shape your trading plan, it is a test of the details.

Then when you can advance in trading, it will be time to move to a real account, as well as online courses and seminars that help the development of trading skills.

4. **Employs strategies and tools for risk management.**

One of the most usual measures to exercise risk management is to calculate the established risk-benefit ratio, which means that before considering any operation, it is essential to evaluate whether it is worth taking that risk in exchange for achieving that potential benefit, based on the amount of potential loss.

The ratio you choose depends on the level of risk you are willing to operate or challenge, it is basically personal circumstances, as well as the type of strategy you are executing, it is also a subject that can be investigated in depth.

5. **Employs stops and limits**

The use of stops is very useful, since it helps to automatically close an operation in case the price has a movement against, for this purpose certain amounts must be established, there are some basic ones that are free, which are closed when setting a price worse than the one requested in the market or if there are gaps.

In addition to the basic stops, there are also guaranteed stops, which are a great help to close operations, they follow the exact level of the limit that is established, but for the use of the same, a premium must be paid, and on the other hand there are the dynamic stops, where positive movements are followed, but they are not guaranteed in the face of rapid changes.

6. **Stay disciplined**

In any kind of cryptocurrency trading, it is vital to demonstrate a high level of discipline, every step needs to be aligned with the chosen plan, so you can avoid falling into any traps, it is a useful approach in every way so that emotions can not take over any step to perform.

The most important thing is to follow a winning vision, so that the operations are assumed with responsibility, the important thing is to be able to maintain this quality of orientation on the operations.

How cryptocurrency trading strategies work

It is generally believed that the application of a trading strategy, produces effect without any concern about its performance or operation, but the truth is that they can be applied manually, semi-automatically, and even fully automated, it all depends on the type of preference of each investor.

In the case of a manual strategy, trades are carried out with an entry and exit methodology, and the results are displayed through the platform, while the semi-automatic ones use platforms similar to tradingview, where buy and sell alerts are issued, everything is managed, even the indicators.

Although the trading actions are to be performed by the investor, until the last place is automated trading, it is based on a 100% technology performance, causing the market entry and exit signals to be produced by bots, following the fair rules for opening and closing trades.

Components of a cryptocurrency trading strategy

For a trading strategy to be carried out, a way of trading comes into play, supported by different elements, such as the use of technical indicators, that appropriate way to read each market movement, it is essential to learn to work with these elements to gain clarity in trading and be successful.

1. Charts Platform

This medium is ideal to get in touch with the indicators, any type of strategy can be reflected or manifested on this space, besides everything allows to program some personal indicators, so it becomes more important to consider these websites, you only need to create an account to use and learn each tool.

2. Technical indicators

Any kind of strategy uses between 1 and 3 indicators, these work mainly to closely follow the trading signals, and there is always an indicator to filter out any errors that may occur.

3. **Seteos**

Indicators have sets, each one has its own configuration, you can not compare the operation with a single indicator, to using a whole series of technical indicators that are chained together.

4. **Alerts**

At the time of developing any operation, it is key not to lose sight of any detail, so most strategies must have warnings to make any purchase or sale.

5. **Levels and signals**

Any kind of strategy model requires the delivery of signals that cannot be confused, in order to have an effective follow up of the entry and exit of the market, this is a way to protect the operations before the manifestation of losses, this also has great utility for the gradual exits.

Each of these components are essential to have an accurate analysis, the operation must be as flawless as possible, but at all times can be adjusted to your objectives to develop a more effective performance as an investor.

How to buy cryptocurrencies

The main ways to buy cryptocurrencies, is firstly under a purchase or by mining, the first is one of the most practiced, instead the second refers to a much more accessible way, on the other hand the second is a scope of a higher level of profitability.

The purchase of these virtual currencies is not far from the investment of commodities, the distinction is on the platform, and currently there are a lot of websites specialized in this function, but this has different classifications according to their management or development of options in the market.

In the case of cryptocurrency wallets, a range of options arises that provide another kind of operation and security, according to the best classification on these two elements, the following alternatives are ordered:

- **Cold wallets**

It corresponds to a hardware, i.e. a physical device through which the coins are stored, it serves as a great protection against theft, but it is complex at the time of making certain transactions.

- **Portfolio applications**

It is a software that performs a simulation as a portfolio, its access is developed by downloading its program on the computer, thus exploiting each of the market alternatives.

- **Online portfolios**

It is a widespread model nowadays, the access mode to them is online, it is only necessary a simple internet connection, it is not necessary to carry out any download, the advantage of this choice is to be able to carry out transactions without any complication.

- **Exchange Houses**

Corresponding to a cryptocurrency bank, the operation they provide is similar to a broker, it is a simple way to buy and at the same time sell cryptocurrencies.

How to mine cryptocurrencies

It is a second way to invest in cryptocurrencies, and it is carried out by being part of a group of people who solve mathematical algorithms, so that they can obtain fragments about the digital currency they are mining, this makes you think about how this process is done, and what it takes to get to that level.

The first thing you need to mine cryptocurrencies is a computer, and when you are looking for a more specialized level, it is necessary to implement a special machine, to this adheres the consideration of the value possessed by the digital currency you intend to mine, since that is the requirement of the power of the machine.

It is essential to estimate that during these operations there is a great demand for electricity consumption, this is due to the fact that there is a large number of people mining, which challenges the potential of the machines, to this is added the estimate of profitability, because if these expenses exceed what you earn, it does not make sense to follow this line.

But over time various alternatives to mine cryptocurrencies are presented, this is known as cloud mining, what is done is to hire a higher mining power over a mining farm, when a high level of power is gained, the higher the profits obtained.

For this reason, instead of focusing on having specialized equipment in your facilities, you should only pay for some that are in another location, but the performance is lower, for this there are companies like Cloud Mining, where the mining power is ceded.

The profitability of mining cryptocurrencies

Thinking about mining cryptocurrencies, not only makes you think about a dedication of time, but as mentioned above, it all depends on the amount of equipment needed, so before doing so, the following estimates are key as:

Equipment and investment for the same.

The level of competition in the market.

Price or value of consumption, to sustain a connection that allows mining.

The cooling required for the equipment to operate.

Based on these variables is that you can make a decision, as well as a comparison on the level of profitability that this option has, but it is one of the second most adopted measures after trading, so it is worth studying the corresponding possibilities to take the appropriate step.

Best cryptocurrency trading strategies

The great amount of cryptocurrencies, are a temptation to try to generate money by investing in any of these, it is a wide opportunity even to have shares of Apple, or Amazon, being one of the most important shares that are available in this market, with so much variety, increases the importance of the decision of each investor.

For that reason, it's all about discovering the right cryptocurrency to invest in, and the best strategy that can facilitate that investment, so to increase your chances of success on these investment steps, these tricks are similar to those applied in speculation with Forex, futures, stocks and other kinds of markets.

These strategies carry out a simple method, as you test them, you can choose the one that works best, without forgetting to keep a close research to the trends, so that you can operate properly, therefore the following steps are very well known and safe to implement.

1. **Buy and hold strategy**

This type of action in the world of cryptocurrencies is based on an accumulation of cryptocurrencies, trying to acquire them at a low price, it is a way of forming a project to invest in some asset that can be accumulated when its value has decreased, which happens because the traders withdraw part of their investment.

This kind of position requires confidence to remain on that asset, until its value improves, it is advisable to choose cryptocurrencies with which you have experienced previously, without overlooking that the reasons for the fall of an asset, is due to the movement of the exchanges, but care must be taken.

This kind of investment can become profitable, as the performance of the cryptocurrency you have in mind to apply this strategy is studied, because not all have a high yield, but are a means to make money quickly, so behind each project should be a thorough investigation.

2. **Breakthrough strategies**

At the moment of trading cryptocurrencies, this type of strategy can be executed, being one of those that generates a high profit margin, as long as the correct actions are applied, this option is carried out in different markets, because it is developed after cryptocurrencies that are in initial stages in the middle of a trend.

The breakout is managed by a concept that is understandable by beginners, as well as experts, where the trader keeps looking for entry points, these are known as those where the price is about to enter breakout movements, either over support and resistance zones going in another direction.

In the world of cryptocurrencies, a wait or expectation of the price is generated, so that it can break the rise with an important resistance, in that way a buy position can be opened at the fall of some support known as base, that is what causes that a sell position can be opened.

The bet within this strategy, focuses on the breakout, as a preeminence of the resistance, until it is expected that the price can descend towards the resistance, which causes it to become a support, for the upcoming expectation of bullish rebound, looking for the price to be close to the support zone, so that volatility grows.

The above situation only means that prices are going to stay in a breakout direction, for each breakout top, future volatility is taken into consideration, thereby increasing price consideration, with double-high, triple-high, shoulder-head-shoulder, flags and triangles price patterns as price formations.

3. Trend tracking strategies

A basic principle that originates this type of strategy is to take into account that all markets have an upward and downward trend during 30% of the time, the same happens in the world of cryptocurrencies, therefore applying a trend following strategy is effective, and with a profitable result.

As long as a trader can enter and engage with a long-term trend, positive results are produced, some market trend can retain its effect for days, weeks, months and years, so this kind of trading can represent a significant level of scale.

This kind of strategy is developed through the study of trends, as they can be classified, until the price is in decline, to allow you to enter to invest, especially enjoying or taking advantage of buying and selling prices of opportunity, as they are close to the highs and lows of the market.

Although care must be taken at dangerous levels, as there is a huge risk of sudden reversals, but in general this practice is very advantageous, to develop these ideas, there are a lot of trading systems, especially for Forex trading, and have a margin of success essential.

But when applying trading systems in cryptocurrencies, one must take into account their volatile quality, without neglecting the oscillations, so it can be late to find the right time to enter the market, those movements are strong, and can demonstrate a false illusion of the trend.

False signals are aspects to combat within this strategy, this happens because of the movement of the market with price range, at this point the mental factor comes into play, because it is vita tolerate certain losing operations, until you can gestate the expected operation that pursues a strong trend.

4. **Dollar cost averaging strategy**

This strategy does not require as much research, nor does it take a lot of time to carry out, it involves buying a certain amount of a cryptocurrency, different intervals are used, it goes hand in hand as the price moves up or down, those intervals are usually set based on months.

This type of selected purchase price can be averaged and is a price point that is either very high or very low, and should result in a profit result as if a lump sum had been purchased in the same time interval, which is a very logical scenario.

The practical example to understand it, is to invest $1000 in Bitcoin, but instead of doing it all at once in the same operation, you make an expenditure of $200 on the first day of each month, that way you can participate within the purchase for 5 months, being a total expenditure of $1000, but the purchase of the Bitcoin is averaged after those 5 prices.

This helps the investor to buy the cryptocurrency at a lower price, for having taken advantage of the months in which its price decreased, this has to do with an analysis of the evolution of the purchase price to which it has had access, thus a technical analysis can be implemented, to ensure that the average has been well done.

To decide on a cryptocurrency, it is important to review the price history during the previous 3 or 6 months, this helps to be sure that the cryptocurrency has recovery options, for this it is vital to choose assets with a long period of existence such as BTC, LTC, NEO, OMG, among others.

In the midst of this strategy, one should avoid selecting currencies that are in free fall, much less that there is no history of recovery, since it would no longer be profitable to opt for that alternative, because it does not have a price range of overcoming previous highs.

5. Balanced portfolio strategy

When looking to make a balanced investment, it is worth considering this strategy, which is implemented through the purchase of different cryptocurrencies, in order to have a much more balanced portfolio, i.e. you can think of investing in more than 3 types of cryptocurrencies.

When having a budget of, for example, $10000, you can allocate $2000 for each cryptocurrency, so that it is an equitable type of investment, also distributing the type of risk that you run with these financial actions, thus proving the profitability of each one, clearing any kind of doubt.

This way, it helps to determine which cryptocurrency class has the highest probability of success, thus, in the next investment, you can bet on only two options by testing their movements, using as a basis for decision the type of profit they generated.

Although the usual problems of this strategy are that if there is a 10% profit in any cryptocurrency, it is reduced by the losses obtained on the other options, but this can also change in favor, counting on more than positive results, it is a distribution of risks.

The best advice to make the most of this strategy is to invest in cryptocurrencies that are anchored to different utilities, be it one coin dedicated to capital, others to security, and so on.

6. Unbalanced portfolio strategy

This type of investment is due to the selection of a series of cryptocurrencies on which you want to invest, then having that clear idea, you proceed to assign a different investment percentage for each one, the difference between one and the other has to do with the value given by the investor.

For cryptocurrencies that have a high yield, a higher percentage of investment is dedicated, for that you have to think about the one that shows the highest profitability, thus deserving to invest a little more, causing the portfolio to be exposed with an imbalance, following the instinct and the research carried out.

The percentages are determined, and used on each cryptocurrency purchase, unless the results indicate some percentage variation, this strategy is ideal for those who love to research every aspect about cryptocurrencies, it is important that each percentage is justified on a reason given by the research.

How to trade in cryptocurrency investment

The investment in cryptocurrencies is developed on a large number of platforms, it is important to select a site that is trusted and recognized, the most demanded at present is Coinbase and Binance, in any chosen site, the following steps must be developed:

1. **Choosing a wallet:** Think about a type of wallet that suits your purposes, the ones with the best ratings are Trezor, Ledger and Nano S.
2. **Enter the exchange platform: Once the** platform to be used as Exchange has been selected, it is time to perform the operation.
3. **Select the crypto:** The crypto you want to buy, you must locate it on the platform to track it.
4. **Verify before:** It is important that before each transaction you can check every aspect, it is vital to confirm the quantity, and keep updating the purchase announcements.
5. **Make the payment:** Once everything is correct, complete the payment from your wallet, so that in a few minutes you can have the selected amount.

These are the simple actions to perform the investment in the crypto world, although you can complement these steps with platforms that carry out transactions quickly, and as for the detail of the payment method, depending on the one you own, you can choose a platform compatible with it.

The most used cryptocurrency investment strategies in 2021

As long as you can learn more strategies or methods to operate with cryptocurrencies, in that same sense you will obtain success, therefore a good way to learn about this world, is following the strategies that are having greater application, in addition to taking into account the market conditions and learn about indicators.

- **Dollar cost average (DCA)**

As explained above, this strategy is one of the most chosen in the world of cryptocurrencies, because it is based on regular purchases, these actions lead to generate an accumulation, where it is sought to make a chronometer of market movements, until waiting for the appropriate mode.

These options must keep a close watch on the level of volatility that exists in the market, so that over time it is possible to measure how much the management of such a partial purchase would have gained.

- **Fundamental analysis**

Fundamental analysis is applied as a search for value, that value that is part of the companies, can be estimated to know how much you can bet on a stock, is an estimate that helps determine whether the current price for a stock, is well below its potential or above, provides a better reading of the market.

When looking at the financial numbers of a company, whether sales, profit margin or others, you can make an appropriate decision, because you study the type of market available, the competition facing the business, this is similar to the monitoring of cryptocurrencies, so behind them are businesses.

That financial structure of a cryptocurrency must be considered, that is why when it comes to practice this analysis on a cryptocurrency, a great level of documentation is required, because that helps to know what kind of asset it is, and above all if it has a demand behind it.

Ideally, the more transparency there is about the cryptocurrency, the better decisions can be made, although this study has become more in-depth, even taking into account the structure of the network and the type of rewards for participating on it, but the basics are to follow the current price, the supply circulating and the capitalization.

The current price refers to a simple element to take into account, as it is the value through which it is traded, this changes depending on the type of Exchange, the best thing to do is to consult a globalized site such as coinmarketcap.com beforehand, in order to obtain a great average on the exchange platforms.

The circulating supply, this is the amount of cryptocurrencies that are in full trading, on the other hand, this also represents the total supply that is available on a cryptoasset, but mostly it is the amount circulating in the market, that is a distinction to consider because it causes confusion.

The market capitalization is part of the current price that is multiplied by the total supply, this element is always observed, because the essential thing is to get coins that can be cheap, that is a growth space to consider, but perhaps then there is not as much upside as you expect, for that reason it is necessary to observe every detail.

- **RSI Leadership**

It is based on the relative strength index (RSI), being an indicator that can not be overlooked, because it has a support of the momentum or the movement of buying and selling in the market, this demands that there is an analysis of the most recent action that has to do with the price, and the price is normalized with a scale from 0 to 100.

Sometimes when the value is low, i.e. below 30, it is understood as an oversold market, and when it is high, i.e. above 70, it is classified as overbought, these measures indicate a price change, so it is important to take into account the role of RSI, as it can be located at one extreme or the other.

- **Rupture trading**

A popular strategy mentioned above is breakout trading, where support, resistance and channel ideas are considered under a special function, these at the same time depend on other metrics, these act on the price action, which helps to understand whether the following is a measure of stagnation or change.

Support is used as a concept that pertains to the area below the current price, as well as resistance, which is considered as a term when it is above the price, that line is generated by the action of different elements such as historical price action, psychological levels, trend lines and much more.

- **Trading with leverage**

Trading with leverage is one of the most successful measures, although it is one of the actions that faces the highest level of risk, it is a type of trading that is developed with large positions, so it is for users who have resources or capital to carry out this measure.

This is a form of business that is generated through leverage, since it is based on a measure of borrowing, that means that if you want to buy 800 dollars in Bitcoin because you have an idea that it will increase, but you only own 200 dollars, the remaining can be requested to the Exchange, to place the rest and the 200 will be a guarantee.

At the end of the operation, the dollars obtained as a loan must be returned, but the profit is kept, it is a way of multiplying profits, but it also raises the risks in another direction, because money can be lost very quickly, so the Exchanges request a reserve as a guarantee.

In this way, these strategies are postulated, which have a great use at present, because they are the methods that are yielding results, and which are also presented as the most profitable according to the users.

How leverage is used on the investment

Leverage is a direct relationship between personal capital together with credit, that is, imposed on what is invested in a transaction, where the investor only has to deal with the concept of collateral, to have access to that amount of funds, which allows to be part of larger positions.

Trading under this modality, generates a great opening towards large volumes, by means of a low requirement, before some high objectives, it is impossible that you count with benefits without opting for this measure, especially when you do not count with a capital to face the operations.

Leverage can be seen as a great opportunity, but it can become a double-edged sword, because the risk increases when using this type of way at the moment of thinking about being part of the cryptocurrency world under large amounts, it all depends on the type of success you have.

To use it, you must have great awareness, but the best indicator to make decisions is to implement a risk management, thus supporting the movements against, so the approach needs to be concentrated on a realistic view, brokers set a leverage limit, depending on the investment instrument.

The smart way to use leverage on trades is to know the number of brokers that open the way to an estimable amount for your objectives, where Broker XTB, Broker Plus 500, Broker ActivTrades, and many more stand out with a level of attractiveness to consider.

Steps for cryptocurrency trading

Before you start trading cryptocurrencies to generate income, it is best to apply a logical order so that you can achieve financial success, following the concepts is key on a beginner's scale, to gain confidence with each step you take:

1. Choose a platform

Thinking about a platform, is to make sure that it has legal regulation, as this works as a protection to operate more comfortably, it is vital to use those that are licensed so that your money is safe.

2. Sets the risk limit

Risk management and tolerance is a limit that helps not to lose the objectives set, much less lose so much money, so if you prefer to have leverage or other preference that generates security, it is essential to have a reading of reaction.

3. Determines the investment capital

Every aspect of finances deserves to be organized, so that investments can have a purpose and optimal care, seeking to achieve the most positive balance possible, although when you have high capital, the greater the opportunity to form a better strategy.

4. Builds a portfolio

This has to do directly with the capital, because when the numbers work as a great support, your aspirations to double the income, become more versatile actions, so you can have a portfolio, where each of the investments to be made are traced.

5. Imposition of loss and profit ceilings

Chance is not a great ally in trading cryptocurrencies, so it is essential to impose ceilings that can be used as a guide to control losses and go in search of profits.

6. Applies all learning tools

Learning about cryptocurrencies does not stop, especially when it comes to technical price analysis, each new trend is a way to create an effective strategy that are consistent.

7. **Up or down**

It is essential to have a posture of expectation, if you will be bullish as an expectation that a cryptocurrency will increase or under short trades, that helps to know if you are trading long or short term.

8. **Attention on the news**

In the world of cryptocurrencies, the social and financial aspect influences, that is an advantage to focus on those operators, it is an appearance of the current situation that the market is living.

Tricks to be part of trading

The compilation of tricks for trading, work as a guide itself, although there is no miraculous way, these estimates are very useful, as they are key points that many traders are imposed as a rule, and prevents common mistakes can be made, so knowing them, increase your ability as an investor.

These tricks can be followed on trading, as well as on any other kind of financial instrument, be it the currency markets, stocks, forex, commodities and much more, they can be oriented towards the aspects you most need to generate income, without forgetting that attitude is a key element.

- Cryptocurrency trading involves taking every process seriously, because it is a business itself, so it should not be a relationship.
- Emotions are put aside when it comes to making decisions related to cryptocurrencies, as both greed and fear are bad advisors, and success depends on having certain psychological aspects under control.
- Investing in cryptocurrencies is a process that requires patience, you cannot think of becoming a millionaire in a single operation, or even on a specific date.
- Expectations in trading must be extremely realistic, otherwise you will not advance.
- Pessimism is also not a help about trading, success is possible with practice, analysis, and never stop learning, because cryptocurrencies possess a very amazing trend of scaling and innovation, there is no reason to give up that income formation without struggles.
- Reading is an essential resource during the learning of trading, especially to understand a lot of strategies that are imposed on trading, when you do not read enough, you just follow a strategy without sense, and it is difficult to choose between any of them.

- At the beginning it is best to try simple strategies, so that they can be adjusted to your trading plan objectives, simplicity is the key to generate income.
- When practicing, you can think directly about the practice or training on demo accounts to gain confidence.
- The profitability of trading does not count on second choices, the basis persists on discipline, work and patience.
- The operation within the trading should be with money that can be lost, that is to say, it should not be a solution itself to the personal economic problems that you have, but as an alternative source of income.

The psychology of trading

The success of trading, as one of the forms of cryptocurrency investment, depends on certain key factors, first of all it is the investor himself, who must perform every action based on knowledge and experience, this is obtained through constant practice and dedication to understand every detail.

But all this is processed directly by the investor's mind, since it directly impacts on the attitude, looking for the emotions to be completely controlled, so as not to lose sight of the right path as an investor, success in this activity is not distant from another aspect of your daily life.

As if practicing a sport, in the same way, it is necessary to carry out a great preparation, both psychologically and in knowledge, that way you can make the most of the opportunities, and overcome the obstacles, for this reason the psychology of trading is vital for a beginner to develop his own strategist.

1. **Fear**

Fear is not a great companion to assume the risks involved in an investment, in an operation, this kind of feeling can be divided in two ways, some opportunity may appear, and because of fear you let that alternative pass you by, it is a way to lose the boldness.

Another situation is that you have an open trade, and fear causes it to close long before reaching the optimal point, so being a victim of fear, causes you to not open yourself to the positive events of trading, which can only be accessed when you allow yourself to lose money.

2. **Greed**

A very usual emotion in the investment aspect is greed, since any user seeks to earn more and more money, but this at some point generates an excessive business opening, which is a great attraction of risks that become unnecessary and even illogical.

In a market you cannot lose control, since this causes operations to be imposed without a measure in between, because there is no patience to evaluate the type of opportunities that arise, so it is essential to be calm, instead of just doubling and tripling the available money.

The keys to put aside these two enemies are the following attitudes developed by the most successful investors in the world:

- **Confronting losing operations**

Spurts are feared in the investment world, when it is a bad moment, one thinks of finding a guilty point or element, to the point of changing strategy suddenly, since it is thought that the losses have been generated because of a poorly made system.

The change of strategy is not a solution in itself, especially because losing is part of trading, the percentage of loss is typical of even the most experienced traders, a solution to this scenario is to maintain a degree of tolerance to the error, to prevent fear from taking over your performance.

- **Sensitivity with winning operations**

A few positive operations are a fair motivation, but it must be avoided that they are a bad example to follow, that is to say that they cause an estimable blindness, because before trading no person is infallible, no one is immune to losses, beyond the fact that no one likes to lose, it is a fact to live with.

Being part of trading is to face a constant risk, so the idea to accept is that it is easy to lose money, for that reason overconfidence is an easy way for negative results to arise, because you take more risks, in addition to omitting to accept your mistakes.

- **Positive thinking**

The operation of a positive vision is key, because that means that there is a high level of belief about the strategy, causing that successful operations can appear, otherwise with negative thoughts are only a direct call for mistakes, by paying more attention to fear.

The positive inner language fulfills a much more effective orientation, because it is a more conscious self-confidence, to assess the facts of trading from a constructive perspective, the best recipe for not failing is to stick to the ideas that can sustain each step.

- **Full realism**

Awareness of what your actions are capable of doing, and what they are not, is vital to have that ability to react to market occurrences, because it is assumed that the market is a great infinity of acts and subjects that cannot be limited to one control, so a trade can have the same possibility of winning as losing.

What you can really control is the investor himself, the way you act personally is what sets the trend on the kind of results you can get, so what you should pay attention to is the way you look for an investment opportunity, and the basis for making certain decisions.

- **Mastery of emotions**

Emotions such as fear and greed, are usual within the investment, but the control or restriction of them, is what marks a before and after, with experience, this is gradually being left aside, the personal trading system should be improving with each result, that is the basic mission.

The solution to reach this escalation, is to exploit to the maximum a demo account, because it helps to create a personal note to have or assume a clear position, with these tests you can optimize your reactions, so you have a better reading on the investment world.

How to trade cryptocurrencies, step by step

Understanding step by step the application of cryptocurrency trading is a continuous flow to develop effective operations under this methodology:

- **Fundamental analysis, after the cryptocurrency of your choice**

The trading of cryptocurrencies in different platforms is endless, for this reason it can be complicated to choose the investment opportunity you have, it is best to opt for the one with the highest market capitalization, in addition to the level of consolidation that develops, or also some of low capitalization are a great alternative.

Faced with this scenario full of doubts, it is essential to carry out a fundamental analysis, where the technical characteristics, competitors and much more are analyzed, to this is added the study of the ranking of cryptocurrencies, to follow one of the most popular paths, the thinking to follow is a potential for the future, along with the current situation.

- **Technical price analysis**

When a cryptocurrency may arouse your interest, the next thing to do is to measure the current situation, not forgetting to take into account the psychological patterns, to align it with the mathematical indicators, to get an idea of the direction of the price, it may be an uptrend with a long position.

While on the other hand, there must be a downtrend with short positions, until the no-trade zone is reached, where studies are inconclusive, each position must retain a sense of study.

- **Market situation**

The opinion of other traders about a cryptocurrency is useful to choose some path, so every news has a great utility and impact on the price, so you can analyze those movements until you gain an advantage.

- **Extra tools**

Having decided on the investment path or route, as well as whether to follow an upward or downward trend, then involves dealing with other alternatives, where the stop loss arises, where the percentage that does not allow losses to increase from that figure is set, and the stop profit refers to the value of the asset on which the operation is closed.

On the other hand, leverage can be applied to increase exposure and risk, up to the intervention of the dynamic stop loss, to be aware when an asset moves in favor.

- **Open position**

Thinking about every detail, allows you to open positions to trade cryptocurrencies, whether short or long, it is an execution to be part of the market, putting into practice the strategies of preference over the investor.

Types of trading

Beyond establishing a trading strategy, there is a deep consideration of the types of trading that can be developed or carried out in a comprehensive planning, the essential thing is that you can make the most of these modalities:

- **Intraday Trading**

Intraday trading is based on opening and closing trades in one day, seeking to generate income quickly, following intraday price movements, since positions are not kept open after the markets close, thus avoiding risks by not keeping them overnight.

- **Scalping**

Scalping is based on an intraday trading modality called high frequency, under this development small profits are sought, through a large number of operations, they are open positions under a trend line that enter and exit the market, these operations are for a very short term.

- **Trend trading**

This type of trading is very similar to scalping, because it is carried out under a position where a trend line is followed, where the objective of the trend trader is to increase profits, but it is left open most of the time, waiting for a convenient price movement.

- **Swing trading**

It is fully dedicated to the price oscillations, this is carried out during a trend, so you can take full advantage of the volatile side that is part of the market, with movements in both directions because they are constantly evolving markets, this causes more opportunity for profit.

- **Position trading**

This type of trading, which demands to be in a position for a period of time that exceeds one day, can be a way to trade for weeks, months, even years, so this implies that fewer operations are performed unlike the others, so it is ideal for those seeking a long-term investment.

- **Automated trading**

Automated trading corresponds to the use of a program through which trading orders can be offered, to be developed automatically, this kind of system has a simple design, as well as complex, the important thing is that they can be customized to meet the objectives imposed.

What you should know about Exchanges

The first thing to clarify when it comes to Exchanges is to expose its concept, it is an online platform that allows exchanging, that is to say buying and selling cryptocurrencies, within this dynamic is also the name or function of an exchange house "broker", which is like an online store dedicated to the resale of crypto.

These online services may raise the question of the type of commissions that are imposed, since each exchange house acts as an intermediary itself, for that reason there are costs to be taken into account, such as the following:

- **Fees applied to the payment method**

Most of the Exchanges do not impose commissions of this type, but when the issuer makes a payment, to buy some kind of cryptocurrency, either through a deposit, or any other means, a commission is usually added, or as can also be a cost for currency exchange, as is usual with the purchase of Bitcoin with euros.

- **Transaction fees**

It is essentially the spread, as well as the commissions originated by each transaction, this type of calculation is generated by the traded volume, which can be fixed or variable, all depending on market prices.

- **Balance withdrawal fees**

When depositing money into the account, as well as buying any cryptocurrency, a commission arises, the same applies to the withdrawal of balance, usually two kinds of commissions are set, the first depends on the payment method, and the second based on the exchange rate of the currency.

The usual payment methods that can be incorporated into the operation of the Exchange, is becoming increasingly broad, among which is the credit or debit card, being one of the most expensive alternatives, because they impose commissions of up to 3%, on the other hand is Paypal as another expensive option, reaches up to 4% commission.

To these methods are added bank transfers, being one of the most used ways, and commissions are estimated up to 1%, even cryptocurrency deposits arise, although it is not very useful to start investment from scratch, but when you own certain currencies and want to exchange them for others, then it is feasible.

How to choose the best casa da cambio for investment

Doubts increase when it comes to choosing an exchange house with room for growth, but it is easy to be blinded by modern advertisements, a solution for this is to apply the following criteria to choose a suitable option:

1. Availability of cryptocurrencies

Depending on the number of available cryptocurrencies a decision can be made, in this regard, not all exchange houses comply, but they refrain to a much more limited number of options, so the greater the number, the better the probability of finding the cryptocurrency that has a large potential for profitability.

2. Commissions and payment methods

The costs vary from one exchange house to another, each one imposes a different policy, so before choosing one, it is an obligation to measure all the costs involved, especially based on the payment method you use, as well as the charge they have for the use of spreads and the disposal of the balance.

To these estimates, the way to pay your coins is integrated, since it is a requirement that the Exchange allows you to use the payment method you have, so it is essential to look for a space that allows you to operate without any limitation.

3. The wallet decision

Several exchange houses offer the wallet service or modality, this means that you can have the acquisition of cryptocurrencies in the same place of the digital wallet, saving any action of registering in any additional Exchange.

4. Security

Any exchange house must be measured under the security factor, this implies that it can offer liquidity, also that it can carry or have a high value in cryptocurrencies of hundreds of millions, that proves the level of reliability, and to this is added that they have offline deposit funds, which have a protection against attacks.

5. Deposit or withdrawal limits

Just as you choose a bank, by the type of amount that it allows you to move, the same happens with the exchange house, the most advisable thing is that it is according to your economic possibilities, that is to say, neither so low, nor so high to what you need.

The best Exchanges to buy and invest in cryptocurrencies

Once you know the fundamental aspects that influence the choice of an Exchange, the next thing to take into account is the popularity, as well as the large number of users it has, each parameter mentioned above is considered to discover the best Exchanges.

- **Bitpanda**

It is a platform with great popularity, allows you to buy cryptocurrencies, as well as precious metals in a simple way, you can invest as little as one euro initially, and find more than 30 assets available, as for customer service, they have an active mode 24 hours a day, 7 days a week.

It has a way of operating attached to secure wallets, as well as those that are offline, does not impose any risk, and complies with the regulations imposed within this area, you only need to create the account, verify it, and make a deposit of 25 euros to think about investing with a large personal portfolio of assets.

- **Binance**

It is one of the exchanges that has wallet included in its services, has become one of the most used in China, and is one of the largest in the world, has trading of more than 100 cryptocurrencies, its popularity is based on offering security, liquidity, and also customer service, is available in several languages in addition.

In the midst of the development of this Exchange it has its own cryptocurrency, without leaving aside that it provides contests, learning material for beginners and much more, it is a way to trade openly.

- **Coinbase**

This is considered one of the largest exchange houses in the world, it operates in more than 100 countries, since 2012 it has been developing services of this type, and 97% of its funds are under secure storage, with different access modalities to make life easier for any type of user.

It is important that before any operation you consult the type of commission involved, in addition to finding the payment method compatible with your aspirations, thus becoming a safe choice for your interests.

- **Bitfinex**

It is an exchange and trading platform available for any project, it is also available for the active purchase and sale of cryptocurrencies in cash, and on margin while trading, although it has a wide variety of assets, its payment methods are restricted to only cryptocurrency deposits and bank transfer.

- **Liquid**

This Japanese exchange house, has a very striking volume of transactions, for that reason it is positioned as one of the best, allowing to buy up to 69 tokens, in addition to providing access to a trading platform, so you can trade with hundreds of coins and is easily linked to the wallet.

- **Kriptomat**

It is one of the best alternatives to be part of the investment in cryptocurrencies, under the credit card payment method, making it easy to be part of this world, it is a platform that does not generate any complication, and is ideal for novice users, as each option is well explained.

- **Bitstamp**

It is considered one of the largest exchanges in Europe, so its operation is important on a continental level, and it has been awarded as one of the four exchanges that determine the price of Bitcoin, making way for a higher level of reliability.

Prediction markets to consider in 2021

Market predictions are anchored to the type of trend that is predominant in the world, this can be the Super Bowl, as well as the final of the World Cup, such impacts to the world, create a broad forecast in terms of markets to consider.

But, it is crucial to know what a prediction market is, this is known as a form of probability trading, everything is estimated based on the outcome of some event, to get to that level it is vital to have a collection of information, as there are many factors involved about these steps.

Although, when it comes to pricing, participation in a prediction market makes sense, that type of pricing encompasses the value of the stocks that are in the market, each prediction reflects what participants will believe or estimate as the final outcome, it is based on a real life event that involves a choice.

Whenever cryptocurrencies expand in a general way, the blockchain technology itself has solutions, and contributes to a decentralized model, which is why prediction markets serve as decentralized protocols to change the outcome of events in algorithms by meeting conditions.

1. **Augur**

It is a decentralized prediction market, which was originated by the ERC-20 protocol belonging to Ethereum (ETH), was developed since 2014, represents one of the base prediction markets, to fulfill that mission of democratizing finance, and in 2018 was issued a release to the public.

One of the key qualities of this market is that it is developed as a fully decentralized model, so that any user is able to create or generate a market on any type of event related to real life, in the same way highlights the currency trading that is developed.

On the other hand, there is the possibility of imposing trading fees and an unlimited supply of tokens, also arises the establishment of an incentivized community resolution system, as it guarantees the accurate resolution of the events that have been completed, thus raising more than 5 million dollars and still growing.

2. Gnosis

This has been shaped as one of the largest prediction markets, and is classified as one of the first dApps on the Ethereum network, in the midst of this market crowdsourcing is applied seeking to determine the outcome of different situations in life, this causes an open market instauration feature.

Any user can create a market based on prediction, it employs a two token system, up to a distribution of tokens over a large centralized portion, it has been ranked as one of the largest fastest ICOs in history, it is similar to Augur, for that reason they are the largest in terms of prediction.

3. **Stox**

This is another prediction market that follows the ERC-20 protocol of Ethereum, it has the same dynamics of other markets, seeking a decentralized performance, in the middle of the performance is allowed the creation of the open market, with the use of the native token STX, it is a useful currency for trading.

In the case of Bancor's token, it has a reserved liquidity, to this is incorporated the oracle and dispute resolution as one of the most outstanding functionalities, but it is one of the most controversial and criticized markets for being accused by means of the Securities and Exchange Commission of the United States.

4. **Delphy**

It is one of the markets built as a social mobile prediction, it is linked on the Ethereum network, its action belongs to the prediction of cryptocurrencies, until it included the consideration of events in real life, and its dynamics possesses a quality of a high transaction speed.

Delphy has its own token for trading, up to the centralized oracle exercise, for each event this measure is customized, it has a Chinese and Asian focus of great magnitude, in which a great ability to create the future is developed, in which all users participate.

The diversity of cryptocurrencies

The estimation of cryptocurrencies is exceeding the amount of 2000, every week a different creation is presented, this process is known as ICO, among the most popular ones are Bitcoin, Dash, Neo, Tron, Litecoin, Ripple, Monero, among others, this is wide and can be consulted up to its legal basis, with a respective quotation.

The proposals of cryptocurrencies do not stop, every aspect remains under innovation, especially the issue of IPOs of different companies, this is striking under the use of ICOs, this fulfills the function of financing business projects, which generates access towards the foundation of new virtual currencies.

This makes you think about what kind of cryptocurrencies to invest in, this is answered under the ways to invest in them, as there are two ways to do it, firstly by trading and on the other is the mining of virtual currencies, this increases the relevance of choosing correctly the asset and how to exploit it to the maximum.

In recent times the most profitable type of cryptocurrencies have been measured, that is determined under the performance of each one, to count on that kind of profit, which can be visualized as follows:

- **Aave:** It has an accumulated return of 6398.22% in the last year 2020.
- **Kusama:** It has a high yield of 5222.37% over the past year.
- **Celsius Netowork:** The yield is around 3843.88% as the latest yield.
- **Band Protocol:** It has a profitability of 2850.66% of last year's development.
- **Theta Token:** Based on 2299.39% accumulation in the last year.

Each of these sectors are driven by technology, each platform is used to make commercial exchanges on a daily basis, this generates that each currency can be placed in a privileged place, this deserves special attention so as not to overlook the opportunity to invest in the most attractive sector.

The most profitable cryptocurrencies

The current profitability of a cryptocurrency does not ensure that it will have certain profitability in the future, that is a maxim of market behavior, especially when the evolution of this kind of currency is so volatile, therefore the potential for changes is the order of the day, based on the most successful quotes highlight the following currencies:

1. **Bitcoin**

Beyond the appearances of cryptocurrencies, the Bitcoin continues to be one of the best investments in terms of cryptocurrency, its birth marked a before and after, so there are plenty of reasons to think about investing in Bitcoin, although there are currencies with higher appreciation, the Bitcoin is the one with the best future.

2. **Ethereum**

This is the second alternative to Bitcoin, it is also one of the second best capitalized currencies, its power is focused on the development or management of intelligent applications, for that reason Ethereum and Ether were recognized as the most profitable in 2020.

3. **Ripple**

It is based on one of the currencies with the highest capitalization after the previous ones, its growth is also a remarkable aspect, therefore it has a high financial potential, and it is not a new or novice currency, but it has 5 years of experience with a base on technology, and allows up to 1000 transactions per second.

4. **IOTA**

It corresponds to one of the most profitable projects, because it leaves a deep footprint in the cryptocurrency sector, it seeks to add a large number of virtual currencies on the Internet, but with the difference that it uses a Tangle technology, being a much more scalable and faster modality compared to blockchain.

5. **NEO**

It is called or classified as the Ethereum of China, the future is estimated on the Asian market, it is an aspect of cryptocurrencies with a lot of future, although the Chinese government has a direct participation on that sector, bursting with the decentralized side that is customary in this world.

Which investment to choose in the world of cryptocurrencies?

The world of cryptocurrencies poses a lot of opportunities to take advantage of, but how to get started and succeed is the unknown, these paths are a largely personal decision, but mostly the preferred ones are Bitcoin and Ether, being the key pillars of this kind of modern finance.

But within each network, options abound, in the case of Ethereum, the alternative of stablecoins can arise, being a cryptocurrency that is created by means of Bitcoin blocks, with the purpose of sustaining the market price, and is anchored to the assets to which it is linked.

Ethereum is conceived as a huge ecosystem at present, it has a great impact on decentralized finance, reaching a value of 43 trillion, thus justifying the firm's choice of this type of cryptocurrency, but the prominent role of Ada cannot be overlooked.

Ada cryptocurrency is an asset with a lot of projection, as is also very striking Lumen, being an intermediary point for currency conversion, it is interesting world with great projects, and each advance postulates a volatile movement, so to overcome any level of uncertainty is key to inquire.

The advantages and disadvantages of investing in cryptoassets

The issues of virtual currencies are not simple, this is due to its poor understanding, because it is difficult for any citizen to be part of this dynamic, much less of the figure of fiat money, so called because it is not backed by any asset, to understand that it is based on a series of stored codes with a high value.

Since the creation of the new electronic money system imposed by Satoshi Nakamoto, the passion for these decentralized methods has grown, no matter what kind of support the central bank has, it is a completely revolutionary idea, the attraction to invest in this sector is high.

The advantages to be considered for entering this financial environment are the following:

1. **Considered as global currencies**

Virtual currencies do not have any type of regulation, i.e. neither the State, nor the bank or any other similar institution intervenes, which means that their use cannot be controlled by any border, but represents a global scale, and their use has been compared to the dynamics of e-mail.

Cryptocurrencies are dominated by the users, the changes must be taken on and imparted by the users, beyond any improvement on the software.

2. **They have security**

In terms of counterfeiting or duplication of cryptocurrencies, there is a lower incidence, it is practically impossible, since it is a cryptographic technique that prevents this kind of events, i.e. each user has a different cryptographic key, causing that anyone can perform digital operations freely.

3. **One group of cryptocurrencies is deflationary**

In the case of cryptocurrencies such as Bitcoin and Litecoin, it is a limited issue that they have, i.e. Bitcoin reaches up to 21 million, while Litecoin reaches 84 million, it is a reduction that is caused over time.

4. **These are irreversible exchanges**

An advantage of the world of cryptocurrencies is that they are executed through irreversible operations, which means that no third party is able to cancel or modify the transaction once it is carried out, this is due to the fact that they are not regulated in any central body, nor is there an access that interferes in that way.

5. **They are assets that have immediacy**

Cryptocurrencies meet the quality of electronic commerce, where payments are developed under a level of immediacy, helping to generate a connection with international customers or users, it is a versatile payment method that breaks any barrier, creating a global exchange process, without delays or annoying intermediaries.

6. **Quality as a transparent asset**

Each transaction made with virtual currencies, are carried out through Blockchain technology, this causes the actions to be public, that file remains in a block chain, and its backup is located in different computers, that storage is available to any user.

In addition to these advantages, there are certain negative elements that should not be overlooked, as they are reasons why certain sectors of society are turning away from this option, every future investment should consider the following:

1. **High possibility of loss of money**

There is no doubt that one of the greatest dangers of this investment world, like all others, is the risk involved, but this is in addition to any kind of carelessness that occurs with the management of the wallet, since it depends on the backup of the password, and avoid hacks that affect the virtual money.

2. **Negative changes due to lack of regulation**

Currently, as mentioned above, there are advances in the regulation of cryptocurrency transactions, as well as institutions that regulate transactions and belong to the European Union, so any legal change may affect the level of virtual currencies you own or the way you operate.

3. **Distrust of users**

Although the cryptocurrency trend has become popular, there is still a high level of skepticism about trading with users, especially due to price fluctuations, as well as lack of knowledge, which hinders the commercialization of these virtual currencies.

The best demo brokers

In the same way that you buy an item thoroughly, with the same approach you should practice investing before taking that step into a volatile world, so that you can gain confidence you can have access to demo brokers, this helps to learn much more, and take into account the features and guarantees.

Before investing real money, there is no doubt that a key option is to test in advance to follow a much safer line, you can get a demo account to help you scale, having a greater familiarity with the functions of a broker, you can start with these alternatives:

- **Plus500**

It allows to practice trading with stocks, indices, commodities, and especially cryptocurrencies, has a regulation to support its operations, allows to fulfill unlimited demo actions, in addition to having access to all kinds of devices, with applications of all kinds.

To have a demo account, you only need to have an email, password and find each option that is part of this software, you can use a Facebook or Google account, so you have a fictitious balance of up to 40,000 euros, it is very easy to use and has alerts of market movements.

- **xStation**

In order to have the possibility to get a foothold in trading, this is an effective option, with a platform prepared for a great variety of devices, the registration only depends on email, name and identity, type of account and password, the fictitious balance is around 20,000 euros, for a limit of 4 weeks of operation.

- **eToro**

The practice of trading with cryptocurrencies becomes a reality through this answer, it has a legal regulation to develop all kinds of commercial exchanges, you can have access from the website, as well as from some mobile device, although without registering you can observe the functions.

eToro's investment markets are very diverse and attractive, the only data required is identification, email, and having a balance of around or up to 100,000 euros, to launch the trading capacity.

- **Naga**

The demo access to the world of cryptocurrencies is guaranteed through Naga, being able to practice with first level tools, with a simple registration phase, it also has an operation for macOS and Windows, it is an advantage to venture with the power of brokers.

- **Libertex**

The cryptocurrency market is open for effective training, and best of all, there is no need to register to find each option, available with a variety of devices, allowing trading with a fictitious balance, allowing the price of assets to be put to the test.

- **Trade.com**

It is developed as a wide opportunity to be part of the world of cryptocurrencies, its demo operation is accessible from any way, and at the same time use all the functionalities, counting with a fictitious balance of 10.000 euros, all this is provided by the demo account.

The best way to choose a demo broker, is to estimate the free side of the service along with its operation, the intention is to have a learning first, the following is to devote attention to the issue of ease of registration, without so many requirements in between, and with an access tailored to you, without forgetting the power of each tool.

Alternative methods to earn money with cryptocurrencies

Beyond investing and waiting for cryptocurrency prices, there are a number of ways to make money with cryptocurrencies, each with its own proportion of risks, possibilities and techniques, and it is crucial to go into detail about these options:

1. **Automatic trading**

In the financial world there are trading robots, being a great option for those who do not have enough knowledge about this world of investment, it is also a valuable way to save time, since it will not be necessary to follow graphs, and the occurrences of the markets, but it is still a risky way as any investment.

It is a series of software where traders can enjoy profits under an automatic mode, are robots that detect trading signals, looking to buy and sell in a space of great advantage, it all depends on the quality of the algorithm, as well as the market movement, it is an important margin of error.

2. Free cryptocurrencies

It is based on a free alternative to be part of the cryptocurrency world, although in general they are not totally free, they are used as part of a PoS (proof of stake) participation scheme, without the proof of work, they are rewards that are usually delivered by means of airdrops.

3. Cryptocurrency betting

For risk lovers, this is undoubtedly a path of pure adrenaline, since virtual currencies have begun to be part of the gambling world, each betting platform is open to chance, through which you can win or lose cryptocurrencies, at the international level, exclusive cryptocurrency casinos have been shared.

4. Charges for professional services

Currently, charging for professional services is done through a cryptocurrency, allowing each freelancer to have a versatile option on their income, it all depends on the negotiations that are established with clients.